Fourth Position for the Cello

Navigating the Fingerboard

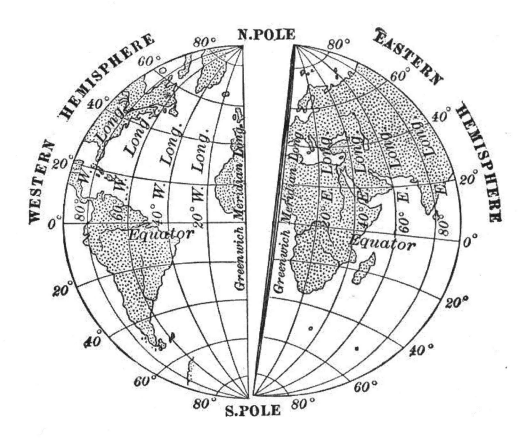

by Cassia Harvey

CHP131

www.charveypublications.com - print books
www.learnstrings.com - PDF downloadable books
www.harveystringarrangements.com - chamber music

Fourth Position

Slide fingers on the string.
Slide thumb up with the hand.

1

First finger on all the strings

C. Harvey

2

Ode to Joy

Beethoven, arr. Harvey

Lesson

Azais, arr. Harvey

3

A string

D string

G string

C string

4

Twinkle, Twinkle

Traditional, arr. Harvey

French Folk Song

Traditional, arr. Harvey

5

6

Old Joe Clark

Traditional, arr. Harvey

Old Joe Clark Variation

Traditional, arr. Harvey

7

Second finger on A and D

Across Strings

8

Ukrainian Folk Song

Traditional, arr. Harvey

Vivace

L. Mozart, arr. Harvey

9

Second finger on G

Second finger on C

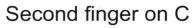

Across strings

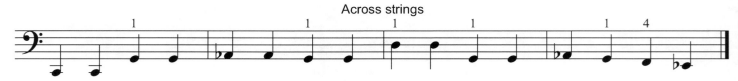

10

Aiken Drum Traditional, arr. Harvey

Polly Wolly Doodle Traditional, arr. Harvey

11

Third finger on A

Third finger on D

Across strings

12

Rolling Off A Log

Traditional, arr. Harvey

Fire in the Mountain

Traditional, arr. Harvey

13

Third Finger on G

Third Finger on C

Across strings

14

Yankee Doodle

Traditional, arr. Harvey

The Swallowtail Jig

Traditional, arr. Harvey

15

Fourth Position Study on A

Fourth Position Study on D

16

The Nutcracker

Tchaikovsky, arr. Harvey

Minuet

Bach, arr. Harvey

17

Harmonic A on the A string

Harmonic D on the D string

18

The Water is Wide

Traditional, arr. Harvey

Country Gardens

Traditional, arr. Harvey

19

Harmonic G on the G string

Harmonic C on the C string

20

Drill Ye Tarriers, Drill

Mary Had a Little Lamb

Traditional, arr. Harvey

21

Fourth Position Study

22

Staten Island Hornpipe

Traditional, arr. Harvey

Autumn

Vivaldi, arr. Harvey

23

First to Fourth on A and D

First to Fourth on D and G

24

Frere Jacques

Traditional, arr. Harvey

French Dance

Traditional, arr. Harvey

25

First to Fourth on G and C

First to Fourth Across Strings

26

Au Claire de la Lune

Traditional, arr. Harvey

Allegro

Harvey

27

Crossing strings and shifting

28

Musette

Bach, arr. Harvey

29

Crossing strings with 4th finger

Shifting from an Open String

30

Lavender's Blue

Traditional, arr. Harvey

4th Finger Dance

Harvey

31

Crossing Strings with 1 and 4

Shifting from an Open String

32

Surprise Symphony Theme

Haydn, arr. Harvey

The Galway Piper

Traditional, arr. Harvey

**Crossing Strings with
1st and 3rd Fingers**

33

Crossing Strings to 2nd Finger

34

Presto

Harvey

English Folk Tune

Traditional, arr. Harvey

35

Octaves

Crossing Strings to Harmonic

36

Minuet

Bach, arr. Harvey

What Do You Do With a Drunken Sailor?

Traditional, arr. Harvey

37

Shifting back to 1st finger ♯

D string

G string

C string

38

Vivace Harvey

Polonaise Bellini, arr. Harvey

39

6/8 Etude

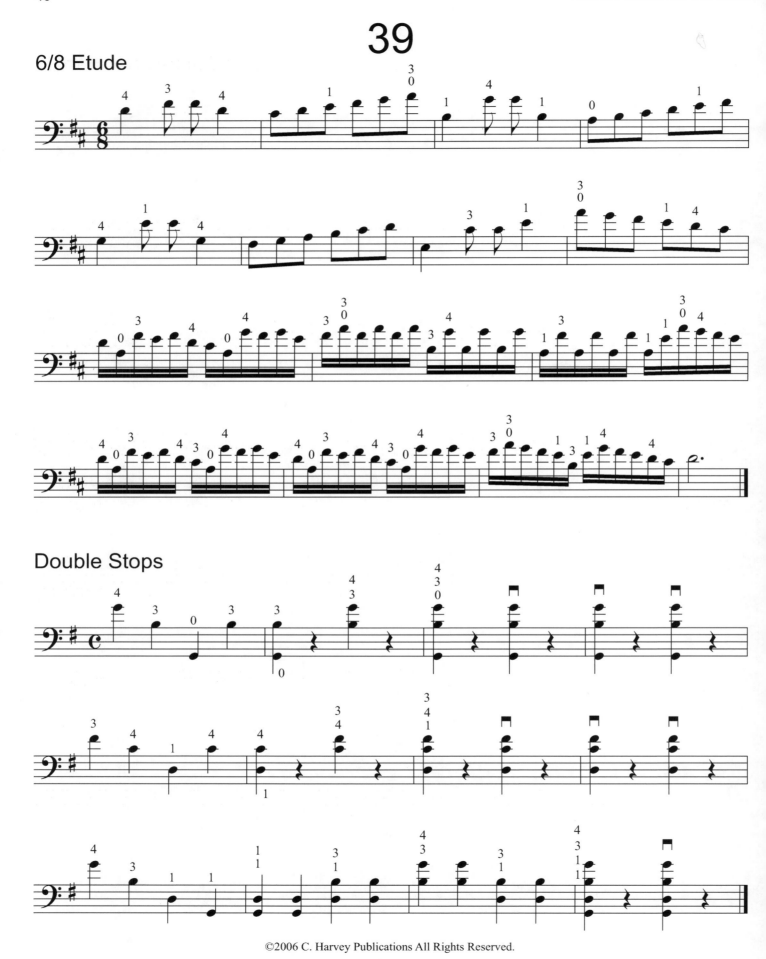

Double Stops

40

The Girl I Left Behind Me

Traditional, arr. Harvey

Prelude

Bach, arr. Harvey

42 Hold each note and stretch to the next position.
Then release the original finger and play the next note.
("Hold and stretch")

Stretching back

42

Hot Cross Buns

Traditional, arr. C. Harvey

Merrily We Roll Along

Traditional, arr. Harvey

43

Shifting back from stretch position

D string

G string

C string

44

Theme from La Traviata

Verdi, arr. Harvey

45

Shifting up to stretch position

half step

D string

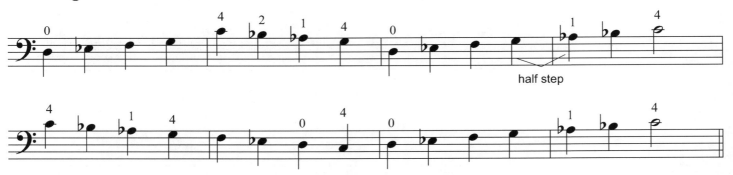

half step

G string

half step

C string

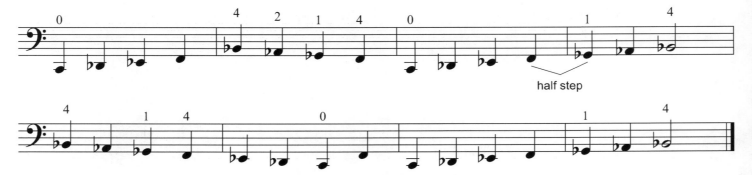

half step

46

A Midsummer Night's Dream

Mendelssohn, arr. Harvey

47

Shifting to E♭ and D♯

Shifting to A♭ and G♯

48

Moderato

Le Couppey, arr. Harvey

Allegro

Brandt, arr. Harvey

49

Stretch position and harmonics

Stretching scales with harmonics

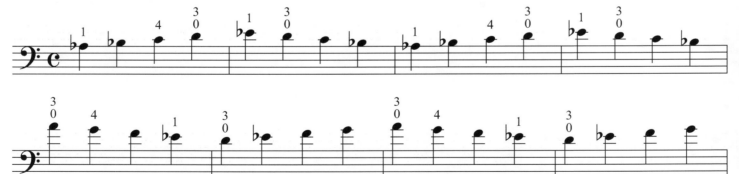

50

Bourree

Handel, arr. Harvey

51

Stretching across strings

52

Suo-Gan

Traditional, arr. Harvey

Fiddle Tune

Harvey

Leather Breeches

Traditional, arr. Harvey

53

Stretching forward

D string

G string

C string

54

Theme from Piano Sonata

Mozart, arr. Harvey

55

Shifting and stretching

D string

G string

C string

56

Polovetsian Dance

Borodin, arr. Harvey

Buttermilk and Cider

Traditional, arr. Harvey

57

Exercise for "Sally Gardens"

58

Sally Gardens   Traditional, arr. Harvey

Can-Can   Offenbach, arr. Harvey

59

Reaching Across the Strings

Rigoletto Exercise

60

March

Bach, arr. Harvey

Rigoletto

Verdi, arr. Harvey

61

Switching stretch positions

D string

G string

C string

62

Concertino

Kuchler, arr. Harvey

1812 Overture

Tchaikovsky, arr. Harvey

High 4th finger; A string

63

High 4th finger; D string

64

Menuet

Harvey

French Dance

Traditional, arr. Harvey

65

Slurs on A

Slurs on D

66

Gavotte

Martini, arr. Harvey

67

Slurs on G

Slurs on C

68

Theme from Clarinet Concerto

Mozart, arr. Harvey

69

Four in a bow

D string

G string

C string

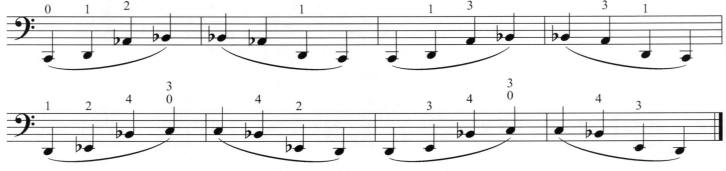

70

Songs My Mother Taught Me

Dvorak, arr. Harvey

71

Shifting from 1st finger

72

Sonata

Branche, arr. Harvey

Allegretto

Donizetti, arr. Harvey

73

Shifting from 2nd finger

74

Air

Anon., arr. Harvey

75

Shifting from 3rd finger

Shifting from 4th finger

76

Silent Worship

Handel, arr. Harvey

Fingering Chart I: Fourth Position Closed

Fingering Chart II: Fourth Position Extended Back

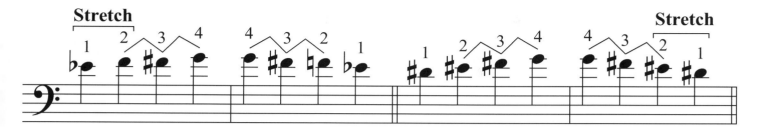

Fingering Chart III: Fourth Position Extended Forward

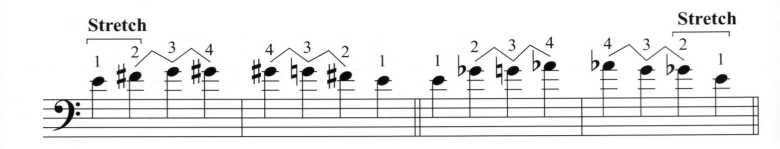

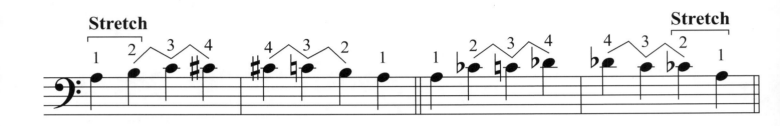

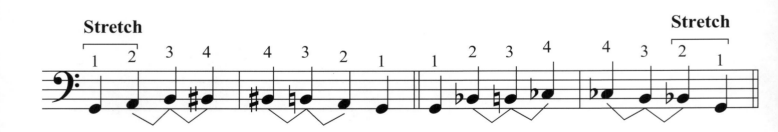

Fingering Chart IV: Across the Strings

Also available from www.charveypublications.com: CHP332
The Bach Cello Suite No. 1 Study Book

Note: The Suite is broken up into sections in this study book. The complete Suite is at the back of the book.

Suite No. 1: Prelude
Part One: Measures 1-4 (Bowing #1)

Suite by J. S. Bach
Exercises by Cassia Harvey

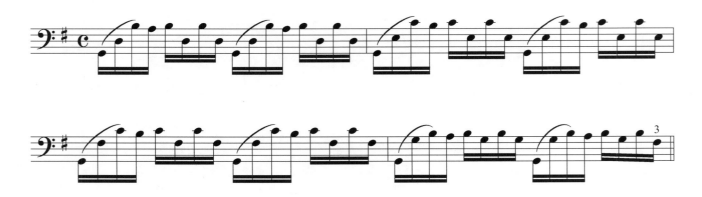

Double Stops for Intonation
Measures 1-4

Made in United States
Troutdale, OR
07/05/2023

10991091R00046